D0866619

Birds

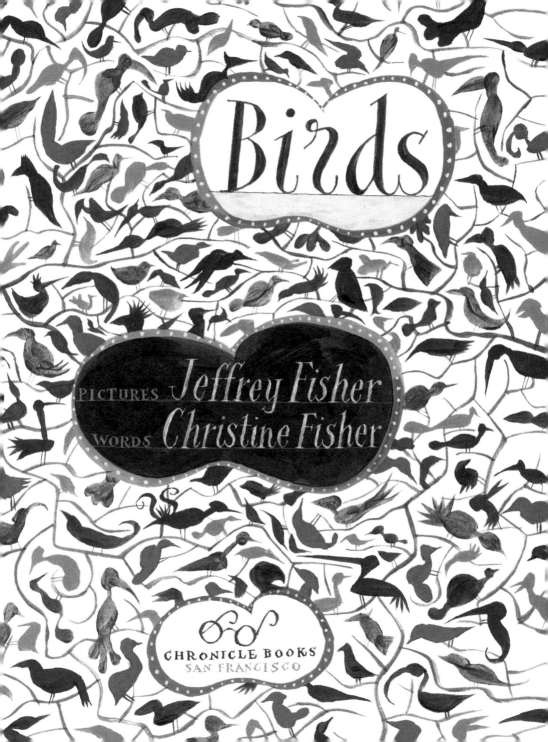

Birds

PICTURES Jeffrey Fisher

WORDS Christine Fisher

CHRONICLE BOOKS
SAN FRANCISCO

Copyright © 2009 by Jeffrey Fisher and Christine Fisher. All rights reserved. No part of this book may be reproduced in any form without written permission from the publisher.

Library of Congress Cataloging-in-Publication Data available.

ISBN: 978-0-8118-6234-9

Manufactured in China

Designed by Gretchen Scoble

10 9 8 7 6 5 4 3 2 1

Chronicle Books LLC
680 Second Street
San Francisco, California 94107

www.chroniclebooks.com

Dear Reader,

This book is nothing but an enthusiasm for birds. There being a bevy of collective terms for our winged friends—a murmuration of starlings, a ubiquity of sparrows, an unkindness of ravens, an exultation of larks, a pandemonium of parrots—here be an enthusiasm of birds. We gaze upon them with envy from our collective windows. They are unmindful of frontiers, direct ascendants from the dinosaur, and I for one wish that I too were a bird. Evidently I have not had the luxury of enough lifetimes to do extensive field research but have relied in many instances on the thorough good work of others. I thank them.

Jeffrey Fisher
Veneux les Sablons

WREN
Troglodytes troglodytes

"Jenny" wren in England and "winter" wren in America, troglodytes
is named for its penchant for nooks and crannies. A remarkably small
bird, its beautiful song is disproportionately loud and far reaching. The
industrious male builds several enclosed nests, and the female deems
one of them worthy of her future brood. This diminutive songster has
a truly wide-ranging habitat and charmingly pert tail feathers.

WREN

LONG-EARED OWL

Asio otus

Widespread in Europe and North America and reputed to have more than 10,000 feathers. Contrary to popular belief and at odds with its name, those feather tufts are not ears. It is skillful as a contortionist; when stretched tall it is convincing as a tree branch, and with wings fanned wide it can appear large and cat-like.

LONG-EARED OWL

NUTHATCH
Sitta europaea

Small, masked climber with large, strong feet, the nuthatch scales up and headlong down tree trunks with dexterity.

NUTHATCH

HOOPOE
Upupa epops

The hoopoe's headcrest is splayed when the bird is alert, with senses sharp; and shut like a closed fan when the bird is at ease. The female and her brood can conjure up a vile odor as a predator deterrent, and with uncanny accuracy nestlings squirt feces at intruders. Hoopoes occasionally adopt a prone, spread-wing, neck-stretched-over-back yoga position.

GALAH

Eolophus roseicapillus

A long-lived and unruly Australian parrot. A flock of galahs is splendid in flight, a deep pink and gray billowing cloud.

Galah

BARN SWALLOW
Hirundo rustica

Swallows arrive in spring, build cup-shaped nests of mud and twigs or reuse the previous season's roost, then proceed to raise two or three broods. They are a welcome summer visitor and are spectacularly busy until autumn, when they leave.

SWALLOW

GREEN WOODPECKER
Picus viridis

This big, bouncy ground feeder has an appetite for ants and possesses
an extremely long tongue with which to extract them from their quarters.
It has a vivid red cap, a moss green back, and beautiful undulating flight
common among woodpeckers.

Green Wood-pecker

RUDDY DUCK
Oxyura jamaicensis

The smart blue bill is a breeding-season feature of the male ruddy duck. His courtship display consists of an eruption of bubbles from underneath his breast feathers. Ruddy ducks are more at home in water than on land. Their short legs and large feet are better for swimming than walking, and they have the ability to swim practically submerged. Ruddy ducklings have a lot of pluck and are independent just a few days after hatching.

ruddy duck

BLUE TIT
Parus caeruleus

Tiny and beautifully plumed blue tits make a moss-lined nest in a wall or cavity for their huge clutch of up to fifteen eggs. They are inordinately fond of peanuts and seeds in winter and in summer feed fat caterpillars to their nestlings.

BLUE TIT

HOUSE SPARROW
Passer domesticus

Male sparrows have different-sized black bibs, and the owner of the biggest bib seems to be dominant in the pecking order. They have been kept as pets, killed as a nuisance, and encouraged to nest in convenient clay pots in order to be eaten. They are feisty and everywhere.

HOUSE
SPARROW

GREAT SPOTTED WOODPECKER
Dendrocopos major

Handsomely attired, the great spotted woodpecker enjoys a varied diet. Wedged in a crevice, pinecones and hazelnuts are pried apart for their contents. On old trees the powerful bill drums out messages and ekes out wood-boring bugs, slugs, and spiders. This woodpecker is infamous for raiding eggs and nestlings of other birds.

GREAT SPOTTED WOODPECKER

CUCKOO
Cuculus canorus

Onomatopoetically named in many languages—*coucou* in French, *cuco* in Portuguese, *kuckuck* in German—the cuckoo sings out loud its distinctive song of spring. Its curious reproductive behavior was not understood until early last century and then hardly believed. The female locates several nests of smaller birds with newly laid eggs, flips one out and speedily lays another in its place. The young cuckoo hatches before the other occupants of the nest and then proceeds to jettison them, thus monopolizing all the food brought home by the adoptive parents. Different cuckoo populations target specific host birds and, remarkably, produce eggs that match those of the host.

CUCKOO

NORTHERN CARDINAL
Cardinalis cardinalis

A beloved splash of color that sings beautifully. Both female and male have tufted crests and sturdy seed-cracking bills. The male is bright red and black-masked, the female olive brown with touches of red.

PUFFIN

Fratercula arctica

Single chicks are hatched and cosseted in burrows on grassy coastal terraces. Outside breeding season their home is the open sea. The loud human-sounding "aaarrr" call coming from that slightly mournful face has made this celebrity seabird everybody's darling.

PUFFIN

SNOWY OWL
Nyctea scandiaca

An extremely large bird, two feet in length with a wingspan of four and a half feet, the yellow-eyed snowy owl is a daytime hunter with the ability to detect its prey moving beneath the snow. A native of the Arctic, it will retreat to the south when lemmings are scarce and change its diet to rabbits and scavenged fish.

SNOWY
OWL

BULLFINCH

Pyrrhula pyrrhula

Eats blossoms, bugs, berries, and buds. The bullfinch has been a popular caged bird, being so very beautiful and ready to sing.

bullfinch

ROOK
Corvus frugilegus

Extremely sociable birds renowned for forming great colonies, or rookeries, sometimes numbering thousands of nests. Of an evening, returning to their treetop roosts, they spiral together in a squawking, gregarious cloud. They have on occasion been observed performing a kind of ritual; in an open field a large number of rooks form a circle on the ground, apparently passing judgment on a few individuals in the center. Depending on the decision, the wrongdoers are pardoned or pecked to death. This phenomenon probably accounts for the collective term "a parliament of rooks."

R O O K

COMMON KINGFISHER
Alcedo atthis

Petite and brilliantly plumed, the kingfisher lives beside rivers and streams that have handy vantage points for fishing. They excavate tunneled waterside nests, lay several eggs, and often have more than one brood. For the first two weeks of life, before their eyes open or they have any covering of down, the nestlings huddle in a circle waiting to be fed. The huddle rotates, and each little bird takes a turn in the prime position facing the tunnel entrance and the arrival of food.

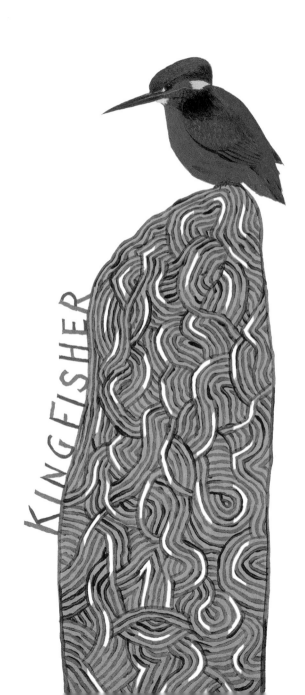

KINGFISHER

SWIFT
Apus apus

"Fast and footless," swifts can fly nonstop from fledgling to adult, landing only to nest in their second or third year. Four toes facing forward on tiny feet can cling adeptly to a vertical surface but prohibit perching on a branch or wire. If grounded, swifts have difficulty becoming airborne. They can fly very high due to a special blood adaptation and have the ability to enter a state of torpor if weather conditions deteriorate while the swift is nesting.

swift

ROBIN RED BREAST

Erithacus rubecula

Permanent and charming companion in the garden, this little fluffy half-red ball with skinny twig-like legs is an irrepressible opportunist.

GREY HERON

Ardea cinerea

The handsome grey heron has an orange-yellow bill and stalks fish by wading silently or standing motionless in both salt and freshwater shallows. Its large nest is made high off the ground. A joy to see at the garden pond, if you are not a fish.

GREY HERON

CREY HEROИ

GREAT BOWERBIRD

Chlamydera nuchalis

Bowerbirds are clever and skilled aesthetes. The male builds an elaborate arbor or bower, then collects and displays colorful enticements in order to tempt the female, only raising his violet colored headcrest when she is near. The female builds herself a nest and raises her brood quite independently of the male and his bower.

bowerbird

PAINTED BUNTING
Passerina ciris

Also called *nonpareil,* which means "without equal." The male is magnificently multicolored all year, and the female is green with a lighter belly.

painted
bunting

GREAT SPOTTED KIWI

Apteryx haastii

Native to New Zealand, the nocturnal, flightless, ground-dwelling kiwi has tiny wings, no tail, shaggy feathers, and a keen sense of smell. The chick emerges fully plumed from its huge egg after a lengthy incubation ready for the night shift, foraging in the dark.

KIWI

WAXWING
Bombycilla garrulus

With waxy red feather-ends, a bright yellow tail band, beautifully masked eyes, and pointily coiffed crest, the bohemian waxwing is very like its cousin the cedar waxwing *(Bombycilla cedrorum)*. Breeding late in the season ensures the fledglings plenty of late summer fruit and berries on which to feast.

Wax Wing

MAGPIE

Pica pica

Long-tailed and boisterous, magpies have a loud chattering call and a good memory that serves them well in recovering their cache of nuts and seeds. They build a bulky nest of mud and sticks with a dome-like structure of twigs and branches to protect the chicks from predators.

MAGPIE

LONG-TAILED TIT
Aegithalos caudatus

The long-tailed tit takes wing in small parties, roosting as a feathery gang for warmth in winter. This extended family can assist in the raising of a brood. The lavishly constructed ball-shaped nest made of feathers, spider-webs, soft dry moss, and lichen has the very practical quality of naturally expanding to accommodate the nestlings as they grow.

long-tailed tit

ROSE-RINGED PARAKEET
Psittacula krameri

This African Asian beauty has happily colonized gardens and parklands across Western Europe and is resident on both southern coasts of the United States—a veritable pandemonium of parakeets.

rose-ringed
parakeet

CRESTED TIT

Parus cristatus

Has a preference for conifers in old forests and woodlands and is an occasional visitor to garden bird feeders. A new nest is excavated each year in rotten, soft wood and lined with feathers and moss. Hatchlings are fed spiders and insects for three weeks in the nest.

Crested tit

COLLARED DOVE
Streptopelia decaocto

All over Europe and plentiful in the southern United States, the collared dove is a successful colonizer, having two eggs in multiple annual broods. It has a powerful, propeller-like flight.

collared dove

MANDARIN DUCK

Aix galericulata

Male and female ducks often differ in size and color, but the male mandarin is in a league of his own. In striking contrast to his grey-brown mate the drake is purple, russet, green, and white; with a deep pink bill; ginger whiskers; and orange sails curling up from his back.

MANDARIN

PILEATED WOODPECKER
Dryocopus pileatus

Old forests with dead and decaying trees are essential for woodpeckers. This large bird is seventeen inches in length and has a preference for carpenter ants. It also likes to eat the larvae of beetles and borers, chiseling off bark and probing in rotten wood. Clinging with strong feet and using their tails as props, pileated woodpeckers drum briefly and loudly on tree trunks as a method of communication. The male sports a red moustache.

pileated
woodpecker

SHOEBILL

Balaeniceps rex

This singular bird with its curious bill stands four and a half feet tall. Once airborne the "whale-headed stork" flies with grace and aplomb over its African marshland home. Waiting patiently on watch for large lungfish to surface, the shoebill launches itself on the hapless quarry with deadly determination.

GOLDEN ORIOLE
Oriolus oriolus

An insectivore with a penchant for summer fruits, the female is much more green than golden. Orioles build a sturdy nest woven between forked branches, forming a cozy treetop hanging basket.

SULPHUR-CRESTED COCKATOO
Cacatua galerita

Accomplished mimic and dancer. Huge flocks are made up of family groups ransacking food sources by day and sharing communal roosts at night. Some of their feather-ends crumble into a fine powder that is worked through all feathers when preening, keeping them clean and water resistant. They are notorious for flying in open windows and pilfering any trinkets that take their fancy.

COCKATOO

EUROPEAN BEE-EATER
Merops apiaster

These gorgeously colored birds are long-distance migrants. They consume bumblebees, honeybees, wasps, and hornets after dexterously removing the stinger, then regurgitate pellets of the indigestible remnants. Bee-eaters excavate long, tunneled burrow-nests in banks of earth, and other adult birds assist the breeding pair in sourcing food for the nestlings.

BEE~EATER

STARLING
Sturnus vulgaris

A murmuration of starlings swooping overhead is unmistakable. At dusk, clouds of birds roll around the sky in ever-changing directions like wafts of smoke or iron filings pulled by an unseen magnet, before they finally, for some reason, decide to roost. They have a waddle of a walk on sturdy legs, black feathers with a green sheen, and a yellow bill—the base of which is blue in males and pink in females.

starling

ARCTIC TERN
Sterna paradisaea

Weighing just a few ounces, arctic terns take an extraordinary annual turn around the planet, summering in both the Arctic and the Antarctic, a round trip of some 22,000 miles. When breeding they wear a black cap and scarlet-red bill.

arctic tern

ROCK THRUSH

Monticola saxatilis

Flamboyant breeding outfit for Mediterranean summer, less striking offseason. This rufous-tailed songbird is a long-distance traveler, wintering in tropical Africa.

BARN OWL
Tyto alba

The barn owl flies slowly and silently in search of its little prey. Although in possession of keen vision, this night hunter relies chiefly on hearing. Its highly adapted wing feathers and the lightness of the bird ensure silent flight.

CROW

Corvus corone

Collectively referred to as "a murder of crows." They are canny and resourceful, respected and mistrusted.

WHIP-POOR-WILL
Caprimulgus vociferus

The whip-poor-will has a wide mouth edged with insect-trapping bristles. It rests, by day, perfectly camouflaged on the forest floor and at dusk, dawn, and by the light of the moon catches moths on the wing. Its call is a loud and haunting "whip poor will."

whip-
poor-
will.

GREAT HORNBILL

Buceros bicornis

After careful deliberation and inspection of potential sites, the female incarcerates herself inside a tree cavity, leaving only a small opening. She then lays her eggs, molts her feathers, has her food delivered by her mate, incubates her eggs, regrows her feathers, and emerges four months later with her offspring.

Hornbill

SUPERB LYREBIRD
Menura novaehollandiae

Unequalled as a mimic, the male lyrebird clears and tends a number of raised platforms in his territory on which he spends much time showcasing his immense vocal talent and superb tail. At night he roosts in the tree-tops. The female lyrebird constructs a large roofed nest for herself and her single chick, on whom she lavishes much care for several months.

Lyrebird

KAKAPO
Strigops habroptilus

Native to New Zealand, the kakapo is a large, flightless, nocturnal parrot. It was thought to be extinct in the 1960s until, thrillingly, a decade later isolated colonies were discovered and moved to predator-free islands. They cover a lot of territory on foot, and the male booms out a call of readiness to mate. There are, for now, only eighty-odd kakapo alive.

KAKAPO